Sandeep
and the
Dragon

by Jill Atkins and Leo Trinidad

W

It was time for bed.

Mum came in.

"Bedtime, Neela," she said.

"Not yet," said Neela.
"I want the book about
the big dragon."

"Sandeep will read to you," said Mum.

Sandeep sat on the bottom bunk.

He began to read.

"Huff, the dragon ..."

Neela was asleep.

Sandeep got onto the top bunk.

Huff the dragon jumped
out of the book.
He got bigger and bigger
and bigger.

"I'm Huff the dragon," he said.

"Shh!" said Sandeep.

"Don't wake Neela."

Huff plodded round the room.
Plod! Plod! Plod!

"Shh!" said Sandeep.

But Neela did not wake up.

Huff swung his tail.

Thump! Thump! Thump!

"Shh!" said Sandeep.

But Neela did not wake up.

Then Huff sneezed.

"Achoo! Achoo! Achoo!"

"Shh!" said Sandeep.

But Neela did not wake up.

"Play with me," said Huff.

So Sandeep stood on his bunk ...

and jumped.

He jumped onto Huff's back.

He slid down Huff's tail.

Sandeep yawned.

"Time for bed," said Huff.
"Goodnight."

Huff the dragon got smaller
and smaller and smaller.

"Time to get up," said Mum.

Neela saw a dragon.

"Look, Mum," she said.

"Where did that come from?" said Mum.

Sandeep just grinned.

Story trail

Start at the beginning of the story trail. Ask your child to retell the story in their own words, pointing to each picture in turn to recall the sequence of events.

Start

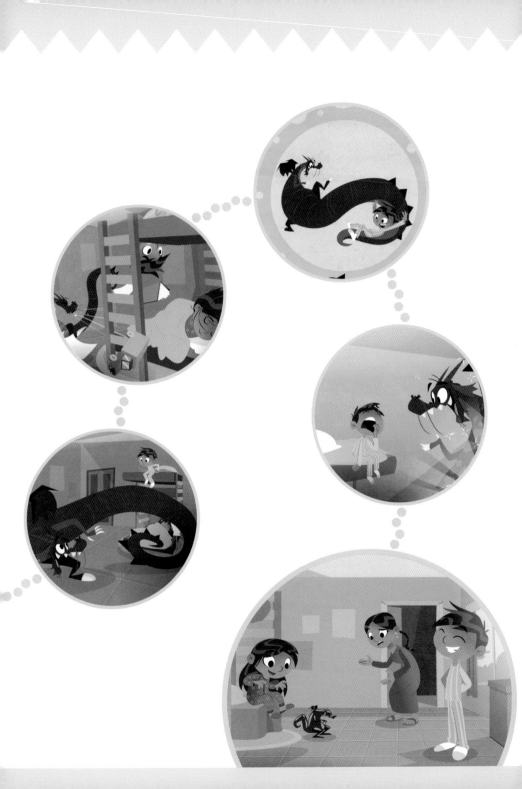

Independent Reading

This series is designed to provide an opportunity for your child to read on their own. These notes are written for you to help your child choose a book and to read it independently.

In school, your child's teacher will often be using reading books which have been banded to support the process of learning to read. Use the book band colour your child is reading in school to help you make a good choice. *Sandeep and the Dragon* is a good choice for children reading at Green Band in their classroom to read independently.

The aim of independent reading is to read this book with ease, so that your child enjoys the story and relates it to their own experiences.

About the book

Sandeep is reading a story about a dragon to his sister, Neela. When Neela falls asleep, Sandeep gets a surprise. The dragon in the story comes to life!

Before reading

Help your child to learn how to make good choices by asking: "Why did you choose this book? Why do you think you will enjoy it?" Look at the cover together and ask: "What do you think the story will be about?" Support your child to think of what they already know about the story context. Read the title aloud and ask: "What do you think Sandeep is reading about? What do you think will happen?" Remind your child that they can try to sound out the letters to make a word if they get stuck.

Decide together whether your child will read the story independently or read it aloud to you.

During reading

If reading aloud, support your child if they hesitate or ask for help by telling the word. Remind your child of what they know and what they can do independently.

If reading to themselves, remind your child that they can come and ask for your help if stuck.

After reading

Support comprehension by asking your child to tell you about the story. Use the story trail to encourage your child to retell the story in the right sequence, in their own words.

Help your child think about the messages in the book that go beyond the story and ask: "Do you think the dragon really came to life? Why/why not?"

Give your child a chance to respond to the story: "Did you have a favourite part? Which story character do you wish would come to life?"

Extending learning

Help your child understand the story structure by using the same sentence patterning and adding different elements. "Let's make up a new story about a book character that comes to life. Who will your character be? What might your character get up to? What happens at the end?"

In the classroom, your child's teacher may be teaching polysyllabic words (words with more than one syllable).

There are many in this book that you could look at with your child: bott/om, San/deep, Drag/on, bed/time, be/gan.

Franklin Watts
First published in Great Britain in 2017
by The Watts Publishing Group

Series Editors: Jackie Hamley and Melanie Palmer
Series Advisors: Dr Sue Bodman and Glen Franklin
Series Designer: Peter Scoulding

A CIP catalogue record for this book is
available from the British Library.

ISBN 978 1 4451 5451 0 (hbk)
ISBN 978 1 4451 5452 7 (pbk)
ISBN 978 1 4451 6099 3 (library ebook)

Printed in China

Franklin Watts
An imprint of
Hachette Children's Group
Part of The Watts Publishing Group
Carmelite House
50 Victoria Embankment
London EC4Y 0DZ

An Hachette UK Company
www.hachette.co.uk

www.franklinwatts.co.uk

FSC
www.fsc.org
MIX
Paper from
responsible sources
FSC® C104740